Journey to the Land of Jesus

A Photographic Pilgrimage to the Holy Land

Contributing Writers
Sr. Alyce L. Waters, RSM
Kathleen A. Marsh

Consultant
Gary M. Burge

PUBLICATIONS INTERNATIONAL, LTD.

Contributing writers:

Sr. Alyce L. Waters, RSM, is director of catechetical ministries at Our Lady of the Sacred Heart Parish, San Diego, California. She holds a Master of Arts degree in pastoral theology from the University of San Francisco.

Kathleen A. Marsh teaches religion at Aquinas High School, San Bernardino, California. She is the co-author of In *Search of Jesus*. She holds a Master of Arts degree in theology from Seattle University.

Consultant:

Gary M. Burge is an associate professor in the Department of Biblical and Theological Studies at North Park College, Chicago, Illinois. He holds a Ph.D. in New Testament from King's College, The University of Aberdeen, Aberdeen, Scotland; and a Master of Divinity degree from Fuller Theological Seminary, Pasadena, California. He is a member of the Biblical Archaeology Society.

Louis Weber, C.E.O.
Publications International, Ltd.
7373 North Cicero Avenue
Lincolnwood, Illinois 60646

Permission is never granted for commercial purposes.

Manufactured in U.S.A.

8 7 6 5 4 3 2 1

ISBN 1-56173-539-6

FPG International: 15, 16, 35, 49 (bottom), 54, 100 (top), 117 (bottom left); Louis Goldman: 20 (center), 31, 34, 106; S. Kanno: Front cover, 66, 81, 87, 100 (bottom); Richard T. Nowitz: 67, 116; Ulf Sjostedt: 117 (top); S. Younger: 28; Jules Zalon: 103 (bottom); **International Stock Photography**: J.G. Edmanson: 50, 84; Ira Lipsky: 20, 44 (top); Stockman: 82, 119; **Richard T. Nowitz**: 12 (bottom), 14, 20 (top & bottom), 24, 26-27, 29, 30, 32, 36, 39, 40, 41, 42, 44 (bottom left), 46, 47 (right), 48 (bottom), 49 (top), 60, 70, 71, 75 (top), 76, 78, 90, 92, 93, 94, 96, 97, 101, 102, 103 (top), 105, 109 (bottom), 111, 112, 113, 114, 115, 117 (bottom right), 118, 120, 121, 122, 123, 124, 125, 126; PhotoEdit: Back cover, table of contents, 4, 5, 6, 7, 8, 10, 12, 18, 19, 33, 36, 38, 45, 55, 56, 62 (bottom), 63, 64, 68, 72, 77, 78, 80, 98-99, 104; Alan Oddie: 52, 104, 108; **Zev Radovan**: 22, 44 (bottom right), 47 (left), 48 (top), 58, 59, 62 (top), 64, 75 (bottom left & bottom right), 86, 88, 89, 107, 109 (top right & top left), 110.

All quotations are from the *Holy Bible*, New Revised Standard Version Reference Bible, copyright © 1990 by Zondervan Corporation.

CONTENTS

INTRODUCTION

In the wilderness of the Judean desert, where the temperature often reaches the low hundreds during the day, wandering travelers may recall from story or imagine in faith the prophecies of John the Baptist.

If you travel by day in the Judean desert, you will feel intense heat and you will see what appears to be endless miles of wilderness. As day comes to an end and night is born, the power of this desert is sharp and cold. It is thought that in this desert Jesus of Nazareth, believed to be the Son of God by the world's some billion Christians, departed to pray after his baptism in the Jordan River by John the Baptist. It is also here that he was tempted by the devil.

The estimated nine to ten thousand square miles of earth surrounding the Judean desert is known today as Israel, but is also called Palestine by many. It is the Holy Land loved by Christians, Jews, and Muslims alike. The capital of present day Israel is Jerusalem, and the official languages of the country are Hebrew and Arabic.

The terrain of Israel has natural variety. There are areas of arid barrenness, volcanic lava, grass, shrubs, and territories covered with mixed evergreen and deciduous trees. It was in this small nation of Israel,

Opposite: This old road to Damascus travels over what is currently known as the Golan Heights. After Christ's death, Paul very well may have traveled on this road to spread the news of the Resurrection.
Left: The terebinth tree is one of the few trees hardy enough to survive the dry, hot barrenness of the Sinai Desert.

Below: *The Hill of Gamla overlooks the Sea of Galilee. Sometimes called the "Masada of the North," Gamla witnessed a valiant Jewish attempt to defeat the Romans in the War of* A.D. *66–70.*
Opposite: *Despite its harsh environment, the Sinai does often provide respite. Freshwater springs in the middle of the desert provide an oasis for travelers.*

located on the eastern shore of the Mediterranean Sea, that Jesus lived. We do not know many factual details about the childhood of Jesus. There are four New Testament books composed between A.D. 70 and A.D. 90 that tell nearly all we know about Jesus' experiences, teachings, and miracles. These texts are the Gospels of Matthew, Mark, Luke, and John. There are also some non-Christian records of Jesus found in the writings of Josephus, Pliny the Younger, Tacitus, and Suetonius. These writings were composed between the years A.D. 37 and A.D. 120. And

Christians also cite the many references that appear in the Old Testament that prophesy the coming of the Lord.

We will travel through Israel to see what it may have been like while Jesus lived. We will also visit the many holy places built around events in his life. We will let Jesus' life lead us from place to place to get a deeper understanding of the human Jesus.

Travel with us to Israel. Picture yourself as both a pilgrim and as a tourist. This holy land can inspire us on our spiritual journeys.

He said to his disciples, "Therefore I tell you, do not worry about your life, what you will eat, or about your body, what you will wear. For life is more than food, and the body more than clothing. Consider the ravens: they neither sow nor reap, they have neither storehouse nor barn, and yet God feeds them. Of how much more value are you than the birds! And can any of you by worrying add a single hour to your span of life? If then you are not able to do so small a thing as that, why do you worry about the rest? Consider the lilies, how they grow: they neither toil nor spin; yet I tell you, even Solomon in all his glory was not clothed like one of these. But if God so clothes the grass of the field, which is alive today and tomorrow is thrown into the oven, how much more will he clothe you—you of little faith! And do not keep striving for what you are to eat and what you are to drink, and do not keep worrying." (Luke 12:22-29)

In the spring, the hills of Galilee are covered by wild flowers, early wheat, flowering herbs, and more. Jesus taught lessons the people could relate to their surroundings, such as this passage about the beauty of nature.

HIS BIRTH AND EARLY YEARS

For a child has been born for us, a son given to us; authority rests upon his shoulders; and he is named Wonderful Counselor, Mighty God, Everlasting Father, Prince of Peace. His authority shall grow continually, and there shall be endless peace for the throne of David and his kingdom. He will establish and uphold it with justice and with righteousness from this time onward and forevermore. The zeal of the Lord of hosts will do this. (Isaiah 9:6-7)

Left: Nazareth is a village in the basin of the hills of Lower Galilee. It was the home of Jesus' parents, Mary and Joseph, and where Jesus himself grew up. Even today in the lovely rolling hills surrounding it, shepherds tend their flocks.

11

The land where Jesus walked is considered holy land by Christians the world over. People today still visit where he was born, lived, worked, traveled, and preached. The humble place of his birth, a manger in Bethlehem, may be the most inspiring of all holy places. The stories surrounding the birth of Jesus continue to interest believers and nonbelievers. The accounts in the Bible are some of the most well-known and most often repeated passages. Both Matthew and Luke tell the story of his birth.

The story of the life of Jesus begins before his birth happens. Isaiah prophesied about Christ's birth and death many years before he was born. Isaiah chapter 9 foretells his birth.

Above and right: *Bethlehem is about five miles from Jerusalem. Modern Bethlehem is built on a double hill and has an altitude of 2,550 feet above sea level. The ancient city was where the Church of the Nativity now stands. An ancient prophecy said that the new king would be born in Bethlehem: "But you, O Bethlehem of Ephrathah, who are one of the little clans of Judah, from you shall come forth for me one who is to rule in Israel"* (Micah 5:2).

12

Below: In Nazareth, Mary learned from the angel Gabriel that she was to be the mother of the Messiah. Nazareth has no history before the Christian Era, but it has since become known to millions of people as the place of the Annunciation and where Jesus grew up. Opposite: Nazareth was small when Jesus lived there. It has grown much larger in the following years because it provides many services for the surrounding towns. It is the largest Arab town in Galilee and is chiefly a Christian Palestinian town.

The 53rd chapter of Isaiah tells of Christ's death. But even in the New Testament, the story of the birth of Jesus begins before his conception. His mother, Mary, was betrothed to Joseph, a carpenter who was descended from the house of David. Mary and Joseph lived in Nazareth, a small town in the region called Galilee. Nazareth still exists, but because of the large Christian Arab community, it has become much bigger. What remains of the ancient village is the old well that continues to be used daily by the women with their water vessels.

Leading a normal small town life, Mary probably thought her life would be normal and uneventful. But it was not to be so. An angel visited Mary and told her that she would bear a child who was conceived by the Holy Spirit.

The angel said to her, "Do not be afraid, Mary, for you have found favor with God. And now, you will conceive in your womb and bear a son, and you will name him Jesus...."
(Luke 1:30-31)

News that an unmarried woman was pregnant must have caused some commotion in Nazareth. At that time, a betrothed couple were technically husband and wife but did not yet live together. The marriage could still be broken apart if there was infidelity. A woman accused of adultery could be put to death by stoning for her crime. Joseph did not want to publicly shame Mary, who he thought was unfaithful. Matthew tells us that an angel visited Joseph in a dream to tell him that this child was God's child and that Joseph should stay betrothed to Mary. The Bible does not tell us when the formal marriage took place, but when the couple got to Bethlehem they were registered as man and wife.

Mary soon found out that her kinswoman Elizabeth was also pregnant. Elizabeth and her husband, Zechariah, lived in what was called Ein Hakarem (known today as Ein Karem), a small town that is about six miles west of Jerusalem. The name of the village means "the spring in the vineyard" probably because of the spring in the center of town that was used to water the vineyards and gardens. Mary visited Elizabeth at her home while both were pregnant, and when Elizabeth saw Mary, Elizabeth said, "For as soon as I heard the sound of your greeting, the child in my womb leaped for joy" (Luke 1:44). Her baby was John the Baptist, who later baptized Jesus.

Two churches in Ein Karem commemorate these events. One is the Church of the Visitation, where Mary and Elizabeth met. This church was built on the remains of other sacred buildings, including a Byzantine church and a church built by Crusaders in the twelfth century. The other church is the Church of St. John the Baptist, a Franciscan church built where the house of Zechariah and Elizabeth may have stood.

While Mary was in her final days of pregnancy, Mary and Joseph had to go to be registered in the Roman census, by order of King Herod. Everyone had to return to their ancestral city, and the descendants of David returned to Bethlehem. Joseph was of the house and ancestry of David, so he too went to Bethlehem.

Joseph also went from the town of Nazareth in Galilee to Judea, to the city of David called Bethlehem, because he was descended from the house and family of David. He went to be registered with Mary, to whom he was engaged and who was expecting a child. (Luke 2:4-5)

Today the journey from Nazareth to Bethlehem would take about one and a half hours by bus or car. For Mary and Joseph, who were traveling by foot sometime between 8 and 4 B.C., this journey probably took two weeks. The distance from Nazareth to Bethlehem is approximately 90 miles. Bethlehem was an important place. It was the city of King David's birth and where King

Opposite: *The Church of the Visitation is in Ein Karem, which is possibly the site of where Mary, pregnant with Jesus, visited Elizabeth, pregnant with John the Baptist. The church was not officially finished until 1955, but the land was bought by the Franciscans in 1679. They did not get a permit to begin building until 200 years after they purchased the property.*

David spent his early years. It also was located on the important north-south route between Jerusalem and Hebron, known as the Way of the Patriarchs.

The name Bethlehem means "house of bread" and although the city stands on hard limestone and the edges almost butt the wilderness of the Judean desert to the east, it is surrounded by deep green fields and lush olive groves. Travelers today see almost what Mary and Joseph saw in their time. The barren mountains beyond the narrow strip of the Dead Sea are approximately 15 miles away.

Opposite and below: Bethlehem means "house of bread." It is easy to see that it earned its name because of its rich soil for farming. Today, Bethlehem has a population of about 30,000 people. Bethlehem is mentioned in a few Old Testament stories, including the stories of Rachel, and Ruth and Boaz.

Above and right: In A.D. 135, Hadrian destroyed the Cave of the Nativity and built a temple dedicated to Adonis. Constantine removed the temple and built a magnificent basilica richly decorated with marble mosaics and frescoes. In A.D. 529, the church was badly damaged by the Samaritans, who revolted against the Byzantine Empire. It was immediately rebuilt by the Emperor Justinian. The Justinian church is the one still standing today.

Left: The manger, which lies to the right of the spot where Jesus may have been born, was probably used for storing feed for the animals. It would have been the best and driest spot to place the baby Jesus.

While Mary and Joseph were in Bethlehem, Jesus was born. Because many people had returned to Bethlehem to be registered in the census, the inns were all full. The only place the young couple could find to stay in was an animal shelter, and many think it was a cave. A church has been built around the traditional site of the cave where Jesus was born. It was built in the fourth century by the Emperor Constantine and a few centuries later reconstructed by the Emperor Justinian. This church is one of the oldest churches that continues to be in use as a place of worship.

Above: *Access to the ancient first century caves beneath Bethlehem is gained here in the Church of St. Catherine. Consecrated in 1882, this church is next to the Church of the Nativity.*

The first visitors to see the new baby Jesus were shepherds. Shepherds watching their flocks of sheep can still be found today on the hills surrounding Bethlehem. But the shepherds on this night were visited by a multitude of angels telling them of the birth of the child Jesus. The shepherds left their flocks and visited the manger and told Mary and Joseph all that had happened to them.

There was a common ancient belief that a new star would appear at the birth of a new ruler. In the Gospel of Matthew, we read that Magi from the East arrived in Jerusalem asking, "Where is the child who has been born king of the Jews? For we observed his

star at its rising, and have come to pay him homage" (Matthew 2:2). In biblical times, the Magi (or wise men) were thought to have almost supernatural knowledge. The Magi were astrologers, not kings as tradition has it.

The announcement of a new king of the Jews was troublesome for King Herod and many of the inhabitants of Jerusalem. Herod did not want to lose his authority over the people, and many others feared they might also lose power under a new king. Matthew's Gospel tells us that King Herod met with the Magi in secret to find out the time of the star's appearance. Herod then sent the Magi to find the child Jesus; he asked them to return to him

Above: *The first people to hear about the birth of the baby Jesus were shepherds, who were watching their flocks. Although we do not know the exact place where the shepherds were, some believe it was in a field about three miles east of Bethlehem.*

When they had heard the king, they set out; and there, ahead of them, went the star that they had seen at its rising, until it stopped over the place where the child was. When they saw that the star had stopped, they were overwhelmed with joy.
(Matthew 2:9-10)

when they found the child so that he too could pay homage.

The Magi presented gifts to the child Jesus: gold, frankincense, and myrrh. The Magi did not return to Herod because they were told in a dream not to go to him. We are not sure where the Magi came from, though we know they were from the East. Because of their dream, they returned home by another route.

Joseph was also warned in a dream to take Jesus and Mary and flee from Bethlehem to Egypt. King Herod was searching for the child to destroy him. By order of Herod, all children under two years old who lived in and around Bethlehem were killed.

The message to flee to Egypt was not extraordinary considering that since the time of Abraham, Egypt was the country of refuge for the Jews. In Egypt, Jesus would be safe and out of the

Right and overleaf: As Mary and Joseph were fleeing to Egypt, they crossed the Sinai peninsula. This area has many barren valleys, beautiful limestone hills, some nonfruit-bearing trees and shrubs, as well as multicolored granite mountains. The land of the Sinai Desert was valued in antiquity for its famous copper mines.

Above: *Galilee is located in northern Israel. Most of Galilee is hilly, but around the Sea of Galilee the land falls steeply below sea level. Galilee was not only the home of Jesus, but also the home of many of his disciples.*

Opposite: *The Judean countryside is hot, dry, arid desert. So much history dwells in this land that when a ditch is dug or a building excavated, relics of long ago eras are often unearthed. The Judean desert and the Jordan Valley have a wealth of minerals, ceramic clay, and lots and lots of sand.*

reach of Herod's anger. The distance between Bethlehem and Egypt is approximately 200 miles. During the time of Mary and Joseph, traveling would have been by foot, with the help of a camel or donkey and at best with a caravan. The weather while they were traveling would most likely have been warm during the day with cool nights. Today, travelers would have the option of motor transport, but the natural surroundings and the views have remained very much the same as when Mary, Joseph, and Jesus took their journey almost two thousand years ago. According to Matthew, they stayed in Egypt until they knew Herod was dead.

From the Bible, we know that the family of Jesus returned to Israel, to their home in a region of Galilee called Nazareth. Archelaus had succeeded his father, Herod, as ruler. Mary and Joseph probably would not have wanted to be in Judea where Archelaus was. The couple may have traveled on the western route, along the Mediterranean Sea. The Mediterranean climate has mostly hot, dry, sunny summers and winter rainy seasons. As they got close to Galilee, they would have first seen the hills of Samaria. The family would have been traveling north, gradually moving east through Megiddo and into the Jezreel Valley. Even today, the Great Plain is where many travelers would be

able to acquire their necessary provisions and continue on with their journeys.

As they traveled, they would have seen familiar sights. Southeast of Mount Moreh is the great ridge of Mount Gilboa. West of Mount Gilboa, it is possible to see the Carmel Mountain range and the Mediterranean Sea. Northeast of Mount Gilboa, one can see the snow covered heights of Mount Hermon, which stands at approximately 8,500 feet. Mount Tabor is east and a little north of Nazareth, and would have been part of the background that Jesus viewed every day.

Nazareth is inland, in the lower middle part of Galilee. The climate is hot and dry in the summer and mild and cool in the winter. South of Nazareth is the Plain of Jezreel. The young child Jesus may well have played on the plain, which was an important area in the history of Israel. Many battles took place there; Gideon and Saul and the Maccabees fought and battled there. Also, armies that had conquered Israel had walked across that plain, including armies of Assyria, Babylonia, and Greece. The River Kishon also runs through the Plain of Jezreel.

Opposite: Mount Tabor rises from the Plain of Jezreel. The mountain is about 1,800 feet high and has very steep sides. Mount Tabor is sometimes identified as the site of Jesus' transfiguration. Mount Tabor is also mentioned in the Old Testament.
Below: Mount Hermon is snow topped almost all year. Melting snow and ice from this mountain are a major source of water for the Jordan River. Mount Hermon is located on the Lebanon and Syria borders.

Samaria, just south of Galilee, has hilly terrain with scrubby bushes. If you were to travel farther south, you would find yourself in the hot, dry, sandy barrenness of the Judean desert.

Nazareth was one of the many small Jewish villages in a predominantly Gentile Galilee. It had fields of lilies and grain, and grass for grazing sheep. Nazarenes enjoyed every kind of fish available for catching in the Sea of Galilee, which is also called Lake Kinnereth, Lake Gennesaret, and even the Sea of Tiberias.

It was in this small village that Jesus lived his boyhood years. There is no reason to doubt that Jesus lived the life of an ordinary village boy of the time. Most likely, he was taught Joseph's trade of carpentry, which was a respected craft. Carpenters in Jesus' day often wore a chip of wood behind their ear to show their trade. Jesus would have participated in the local village activities. He probably began school when he was six; every boy was required to attend. School would have been held in the synagogue, and the teacher would have been a rabbi. At home, the family probably spoke Aramaic, but school lessons were taught in Hebrew.

Life in ancient Israel revolved around the family. Extended family frequently lived in one home. Jewish houses over the centuries changed little. They were simple boxlike structures of brick or stone with outside stairs leading to a

Left: *Samaria was a region south of Galilee, but it was also the capital of Israel until the Assyrian conquest in 723 B.C. Samaria was a place where pagan religions were practiced.*

Above: *Samaria was rebuilt by Herod the Great and was renamed Sebaste during New Testament times. The Jews that remained in Samaria, even though they claimed to worship God, were hated by the Jews in Judea, and one of Jesus' most powerful stories is about the good Samaritan.*

flat roof. It was common for most houses to have an adjoining courtyard with a door leading into it. The courtyard area was used as a work space for cooking, baking, washing, and it served as a pen for the goats and sheep.

On the inside, houses were usually dark and had poor ventilation. Most houses were split into two levels. The higher level included a sitting area for visiting, a storeroom, and a winter bedroom. It is most likely that Joseph, Mary, and Jesus had this type of house.

The Bible tells us that Mary and Joseph followed Jewish custom and fulfilled Jewish law regarding the circumcision and naming of Jesus (when Jesus was eight days old). They also went to Jerusalem to sacrifice for Mary's cleansing, a ritual that followed childbirth.

Right: Jerusalem suffered troubled times after the death of King Herod. It was ruled by Roman procurators, and the Jewish people struggled for their freedom. The Roman army completely destroyed the city in A.D. 70, and the Roman Emperor Hadrian began destroying all religious shrines by building pagan temples over them about A.D. 135.

Opposite: The Sea of Galilee not only provided food for Nazarenes, but it also provided Jesus with one of his only places to retreat later in his life.

It was Jewish custom each year to go to Jerusalem for the feast of Passover. Luke records that when Jesus was about 12, he and his parents journeyed to Jerusalem to celebrate the feast. After the quiet of a small town, it must have been exciting for the boy Jesus to see the hustle and bustle of the larger city of Jerusalem. People from all over came to Jerusalem for Passover; they would have worn different kinds of clothing and spoken many different languages. Roman guards would also have been all over the city, trying to keep order.

The father and son, Joseph and Jesus, would have gone to the temple while Mary prepared the Passover feast. The temple would have been crowded with many people. First the father and son would have gone through the Court of Gentiles, where buying, selling, and money-changing was going on. Then they would have entered and gone through the Court of Women to the Court of Israel, where only Jewish males were allowed. Joseph would probably have bought a one-year-old lamb for sacrificing.

When the celebrations were over, Jesus was not in the caravan returning to Galilee, unknown to Mary and Joseph. Having discovered that Jesus was absent, Mary and Joseph returned to Jerusalem and after three days found Jesus questioning and speaking with the temple teachers. All who heard the young boy were amazed at his understanding. But his parents were not as pleased.

Unfortunately, the Gospel writers do not give us much detail about Jesus' early years, though it is likely he lived the normal life of a boy and young man in Nazareth. We are only told that after the temple incident, he was obedient.

⟨⟨HIS MINISTRY⟩⟩

The voice of one crying out in the wilderness:"Prepare the way of the Lord, make his paths straight. Every valley shall be filled, and every mountain and hill shall be made low, and the crooked shall be made straight, and the rough ways made smooth; and all flesh shall see the salvation of God." (Luke 3:4-6)

Above: *The olive tree is the most common tree in Palestine.*
Right: *The mountains of the Judean desert are where Jesus was tempted three times by the devil.*

Left: *The Jordan River site that is probably where John the Baptist baptized Jesus.*
Above: *In the harsh, dry desert of Judea, very little survives, except a few hardy plants.*

In the desert of Judea, in the barren region northwest of the Dead Sea, John the Baptist preached of the one who would baptize "with the Holy Spirit and fire" (Luke 3:16). John was a prophet who ate wild honey, lived off the land, and wore clothing made of camel's hair. Many people traveled to see John and to be baptized by him in the Jordan River.

Then the people of Jerusalem and all Judea were going out to him, and all the region along the Jordan, and they were baptized by him in the river Jordan, confessing their sins. (Matthew 3:5-6)

The Jordan River is the only large flowing body of water in Palestine. It flows south from its headwaters in the region of Mount Hermon to the northern end of the Dead Sea. The River Jordan twists and bends its way through this deep north-south valley.

The Jordan River is the site of the first story we hear about the adult Jesus. Jesus went to the Jordan to be baptized by his cousin, John the Baptist. John was the son of Elizabeth, Mary's kinswoman. After the baptism, the heavens opened and the Spirit of God came down in the form of a dove. "And a voice from heaven said, 'This is my Son, the Beloved, with whom I am well pleased'" (Matthew 3:17). All four Gospels tell of the dove descending and the voice of God proclaiming Jesus as his son.

After his baptism, Jesus withdrew to the stark, hilly wilderness of Judea. He stayed there for 40 days and nights,

and he fasted. Matthew tells us that the Spirit led him to the desert, and while he was there he was tempted by the devil three times. Each temptation was rejected by Jesus, who told the devil, "Away with you, Satan! for it is written, 'Worship the Lord your God, and serve only him'" (Matthew 4:10). Once the devil left, angels came to take care of Jesus.

Returning from the wilderness, Jesus worked alongside John the Baptist for a while. Later he learned that John the Baptist had been arrested. After hearing this, Jesus left Judea and traveled north to live in Capernaum, which is by the Sea of Galilee. In the Bible, this area was known as the "Land of Zebulun, land of Naphtali, on the road by the sea, across the Jordan, Galilee of the Gentiles" (Matthew 4:15). It was in Capernaum that Jesus began to preach.

In Jesus' day, Capernaum was an important regional city. It was situated along the lake (Sea of Galilee), so it served as a distribution point for the farmers in the area, as well as a port for fishing. Jesus spent so much of his active ministry time in this area that Matthew referred to Capernaum as Jesus' own town. "And after getting into a boat he crossed the sea and came to his own town" (Matthew 9:1).

Present day Capernaum is an archaeological site. Tourists can see a well-preserved and partly restored synagogue that dates from the second or third century A.D., although the basalt foundation is from the time of Jesus. There is also a fifth century A.D. church that is said to enclose Peter's house, where Jesus often stayed.

At the beginning of his ministry, and while he lived in Capernaum, Jesus began choosing his disciples. Walking along the Sea of Galilee, he called two brothers who were fishing, Simon Peter and Andrew. Walking further, he found

Right: On the northwest shore of the Sea of Galilee is the town of Capernaum. During Jesus' teaching years in Galilee, this town was his base. Capernaum was also the hometown of Matthew (Levi) the tax collector. It was in Capernaum that Jesus healed the servant of a Roman army officer.

Above: A Jewish symbol in stone at Capernaum.
Right: During Jewish captivity in Babylon, the Jews had no temple. Until then, their religion had centered around the temple. People gathered in private homes for instruction and devotion. This is how synagogues developed.

Above: The synagogue became the center of Jewish worship and instruction. On the Sabbath and on feast days and holy days, faithful Jews gathered at the synagogue. In Capernaum, Mark records that Jesus cured a demoniac and taught with authority in the synagogue.
Right: This passageway leads into the synagogue at Capernaum.

two other brothers who were mending their nets with their father, Zebedee. These two brothers, James and John, also left their boat and followed Jesus.

Jesus spent a great part of his public life around the Sea of Galilee, which is actually a lake. It is approximately 13 miles long and, at its widest measure, about 7 miles wide. The depth of the lake is estimated at 680 feet below the level of the Mediterranean Sea.

In Cana, Jesus performed his first miracle. Cana was also the home of Nathanael, another of Jesus' disciples. The traditional site of Cana is approximately 15 miles west of the Sea of Galilee. The Gospel of John notes that Jesus and his disciples attended a wedding feast there along with the mother of Jesus. Jewish wedding feasts often lasted 7 to 14 days. They were frequently held in autumn because crops were already harvested and the nights were still warm. It was customary to serve the good wine first, and after the guests had drunk freely, the groom would have his headwaiter serve an inferior wine. However, at this wedding feast, the groom ran short of wine. The mother of Jesus called on her

Left: *Northwest of Nazareth in lower Galilee is the village of Kafr Kenna, which some think is the Cana mentioned in the Bible. Surrounding Kafr Kenna is fertile farmland, and in the spring, wheat adds a colorful touch of yellow to the fields.*
Above: *The facade of the Church of the Miracle.*

son for help. Jesus told the waiters to fill the water jars that were there for the Jewish ceremonial washing. After the jars were filled, Jesus told them to draw some out and give it to the headwaiter for tasting. The headwaiter immediately asked the groom why he had saved the good wine until then.

Today, the town of Cana is sometimes identified as Kafr Kenna.

Above: *The Church of the Miracle was built over the well where the water changed into wine was supposed to have been drawn. This village was already a pilgrimage site in the third century, when St. Paula and St. Eustochium visited it.*

Above: *It was Jewish custom at large feasts to provide vats of water to be used for the purification ritual before meals. Although the date of this vessel is unknown, it would be similar to the water vessels that Jesus requested at the wedding feast of Cana.*

The Church of the Miracle was built by Franciscans over the well where the water was supposed to have been drawn. There is also a water jar in the church that is said to have been used in this miraculous event. At another time, Jesus also cured the royal official's son in Cana. Today, however, most scholars believe that the site of ancient Cana is Khirbet Qana, nine miles north of Nazareth.

After the wedding feast, Jesus, his disciples, and Mary returned to Capernaum. The people of Capernaum witnessed many of Jesus' miracles, including the alderman's daughter being brought back to life and the centurion's son healed.

The people of Capernaum were surely also witnesses to some of Jesus' most famous sermons. Though archaeologists and historians do not claim to know exactly where the Sermon on the Mount took place, it may have been a little north of Capernaum, on a prominent hill that overlooks the lake. An Italian convent has been built on the site, which is known as the Mount of the Beatitudes.

In the Gospels of Matthew and Luke, we read about the Sermon on the Mount. As was Jesus' custom, he had gone to the mountain to pray. Matthew reports that crowds followed and Jesus began to teach them and the disciples. This sermon has some of the most beautiful and comforting words Christ uttered.

Left: *The Church of the Beatitudes commemorates the powerful sermon of Jesus recorded in Matthew chapter 5. The church was built north of Capernaum on a hill overlooking the Sea of Galilee. This hill is frequently called the Mount of the Beatitudes.*

Above and left: The Church of the Beatitudes was built in 1937 and designed by the Italian architect Antonio Barlozzi. The building is octagonal, and each wall has a stained glass window that has the beginning of one of the Beatitudes inscribed on it.

Blessed are the poor in spirit, for theirs is the kingdom of heaven. Blessed are those who mourn, for they will be comforted. Blessed are the meek, for they will inherit the earth. Blessed are those who hunger and thirst for righteousness, for they will be filled. Blessed are the merciful, for they will receive mercy. Blessed are the pure in heart, for they will see God. Blessed are the peacemakers, for they will be called children of God. Blessed are those who are persecuted for righteousness' sake, for theirs is the kingdom of heaven. Blessed are you when people revile you and persecute you and utter all kinds of evil against you falsely on my account. Rejoice and be glad, for your reward is great in heaven, for in the same way they persecuted the prophets who were before you.
(Matthew 5:3-12)

Right: *The mosaic floor of the Church of the Beatitudes is adorned with symbols of the seven virtues that are mentioned in the Sermon on the Mount.*

50

Though there surely were some people from Capernaum in the crowds that followed Jesus wherever he went, his preaching soon attracted people from many towns. There were times Jesus tried to get away to be by himself, such as when he heard the news that John the Baptist had been killed. Then, he went out on the lake by himself, but the crowds found out and followed him. He took compassion on them and healed their sick. Because it was getting late, the disciples asked Jesus to tell the people to go to town to buy food for themselves. But Jesus instead performed the miracle of the feeding of thousands recorded in Matthew.

Then he ordered the crowds to sit down on the grass. Taking the five loaves and the two fish, he looked up to heaven, and blessed and broke the loaves, and gave them to the disciples, and the disciples gave them to the crowds. And all ate and were filled; and they took up what was left over of the broken pieces, twelve baskets full. And those who ate were about five thousand men, besides women and children.
(Matthew 14:19-21)

Right: *Fish was the staple food for most who lived around the Sea of Galilee. Fishing boats still line the lake's shores.*

Today, the site where this happened is called Tabgha. The name is an Arab version of a Greek word that means "seven fountains." In the area, there may have been sulphurous springs. The Church of the Loaves and Fishes was built over a destroyed fifth century Byzantine church. The current church is famous for its exquisite mosaics, especially of the basket and fish.

Luke tells of another time that Jesus fed five thousand with just a few loaves and two fish, this time in the city of Bethsaida. The apostles Peter, Andrew, and Philip were also from Bethsaida. Today travelers journeying to the Jordan River may notice areas of marsh with abundant reeds and different grasses. At the river, around the Sea of Galilee, there is a great descent through rocky gorges, and toward the north, the river slows to cross a plain near Bethsaida. This is where Jesus healed a blind man.

Above and opposite: The current Church of the Loaves and Fishes was built over a fifth century Byzantine church. The Benedictine monks discovered the old churches during excavations and built the newest church in 1936. This church preserves one of the most beautiful ancient mosaic floors in all Israel.

This part of the Sea of Galilee is in the district of Bethsaida, home of Peter and Andrew. It is easy to see why Jesus would have chosen to go out on the lake when he needed solitude.

Above: As a boy, Jesus, along with the other boys of the village, would have heard stirring stories of the great heroes of Israel in the synagogue. This ancient synagogue in Nazareth may be similar to the one visited by Jesus.

Above: Nazareth is the town where Jesus spent much of his life. Nazareth sits southeast of the Sea of Galilee.
Opposite: When Jesus returned to Nazareth and angered the people, they took him to a mountain to throw him off. The story in Luke's Gospel does not tell where the event happened. Some Catholics and Protestants believe that it was Mount of the Leap, sometimes called Mount of Precipitation.

Throughout the Gospels, we read that Jesus was active in the temple while in Jerusalem. Matthew records two particular temple situations. One is the time when the pharisees were questioning Jesus about the lawfulness of curing on the Sabbath. Jesus responded to them with a question, "Suppose one of you has only one sheep and it falls into a pit on the sabbath; will you not lay hold of it and lift it out?" (Matthew 12:11). On another occasion after his triumphal entry into Jerusalem, Jesus expressed his anger in the temple, drove out the buyers and the sellers, and declared the temple a house of prayer.

At one point, Jesus returned to his native Nazareth. He began teaching in the synagogue there, and the people were amazed at his gracious words. Hearing him speak, the people questioned one another, asking, "Is not this Joseph's son?" (Luke 4:22). But then Jesus said, "Truly I tell you, no prophet is accepted in the prophet's hometown" (Luke 4:24). The people were angered and they drove him out of town and took him to a hill to throw him off. "But he passed through the midst of them and went on his way" (Luke 4:30). This precipice is just outside of Nazareth. Matthew wrote that Jesus did not work many miracles in Nazareth because of the people's lack of faith.

In Nazareth, located about 85 miles north of Jerusalem, many of the sites relating to the life of Jesus have been marked. About 1,200 feet above sea level, Nazareth is situated on a beautiful green plateau dotted with white limestone houses. Jesus left Nazareth and continued with his

preaching, teaching, and miracle-working.

At Nain, a Galilean village at the edge of the Jezreel Valley, about eight miles from Nazareth, Luke records that Jesus raised a young man to life and returned him to his mother. The exact number of miracles performed by Jesus is not known. Jesus not only healed the sick and raised the dead, but he also drove out demons. Matthew, Mark, and

Luke report the exorcism of two demoniacs by Jesus in Gergesa. The expelled demons entered a herd of swine, which plunged into a lake. In the district of Tyre and Sidon, Matthew and Mark report that Jesus released the demon of the possessed daughter of a Syro-Phoenician woman. Tyre was located on the mainland and Sidon was an ancient Canaanite seaport about 20 miles north of Tyre. The Bible notes that when Jesus visited any area, many people traveled to see and hear him.

They came to Bethsaida. Some people brought a blind man to him and begged him to touch him. He took the blind man by the hand and led him out of the village; and when he had put saliva on his eyes and laid his hands on him, he asked him, "Can you see anything?" And the man looked up and said, "I can see people, but they look likes trees, walking." Then Jesus laid his hands on his eyes again; and he looked intently and his sight was restored, and he saw everything clearly.
(Mark 8:22-25)

Left: Mount Tabor is more impressive in appearance than its low height would suggest. Only small vehicles can make their way up its winding, difficult road. The view from the top of the mountain is spectacular; you can see all of Lower Galilee.

61

Above and opposite:
The Pool of Bethesda was an open-air reservoir that was built in Jerusalem to provide water to the growing city. It is located right inside of St. Stephen's Gate, also known as the Lions Gate. It is the site of one of Jesus' most famous miracles. The water was supposed to have healing powers. Jesus saw a man there who had been unable to walk for 38 years and Jesus told the man to rise up and walk.

Right: Another part of the Bethesda Pool excavations shows how complicated the site is. Bethesda may mean "house of mercy," a fitting designation for a healing sanctuary.

Jesus also performed miracles over nature. At the Sea of Galilee, Simon Peter, James, and John fished all night and still had empty fishnets. Jesus told Peter to go out to the deep of the lake and try again. Peter followed Jesus' direction and the catch was so great that they had to call for a second boat to bring it into shore. We also read that Jesus walked across the water to meet Peter. When Peter saw Jesus, he too walked on the water until he realized what he was doing, then he promptly sank.

In Capernaum, when the tax collectors approached Peter to pay the temple tax, Jesus told Peter, ". . . go to the sea and cast a hook; take the first fish that comes up; and when you open its mouth, you will find a coin; take that and give it to them for you and me" (Matthew 17:27).

Above: *These coins were minted during Pontius Pilate's reign and were the Roman Standard.*

Once when he entered Jerusalem, Jesus cursed a fig tree to symbolize his displeasure with the temple. When he was going to the city in the morning, he was hungry. Seeing a fig tree by the road, he went over to it, but found nothing on it but leaves. And he said to

Right: *The Sea of Galilee is not always calm and peaceful. In fact, fishers must often watch because storms over the lake can appear very quickly and be quite dangerous.*

64

it, "'May no fruit ever come from you again!' And the fig tree withered at once" (Matthew 21:19).

The majority of the miracles Jesus did were for healing, but Jesus was not just a miracle worker. He was also a teacher. As a teacher, Jesus was a great storyteller. Many of the parables told by Jesus are recorded in the Bible. These parables were used to teach spiritual lessons.

Mark records the parable of the Sower. For the people of Galilee, it would be easy to see the various types of soil that Jesus refers to in this parable. Farming was a common practice then and now. To Jesus' audience, it was easy to imagine paths that meandered through a field where the birds could eat the sown seeds, or a

thin covering of earth over a rocky ledge with thorn bushes, or the good rich earth that could yield more than what was sown. Many in fact dealt daily with those very real farming problems.

There are many other parables told by Jesus and recorded in the Bible: the Mustard Seed, the Yeast, the Lost Son, and more. The parable of the Mustard Seed, found in Matthew, Mark, and Luke, was a story told by Jesus when he was speaking about the kingdom of God. Jesus reminded the people how the tiny mustard seed grows into a great plant. The mustard plant was and is plentiful throughout Galilee. The black mustard seed surrounded by yellow flower petals was used for oil as well as for flavoring. Generally the mustard plant is about four feet tall.

However, they can grow as tall as 15 feet.

Mark does not record the parable of the Yeast. However, both Matthew and Luke include it following the parable of the Mustard Seed. Again Jesus is speaking about the kingdom of God. This time he uses the analogy of yeast being added to an enormous amount of wheat, enough to feed approximately one hundred people. In Jesus' day, wheat made the best flour and bread. It was used to make the bread the priests offered to God.

Only Luke records the parable of the Lost Son, also called the Prodigal Son. In this parable, Jesus illustrates his concern for people who are lost and God's love of the repentant sinner.

A rich man's youngest son took his share of the family inheritance and squandered it on foolish pleasures. When he was broke and in despair, he returned home to a father who welcomed him with a kiss and an embrace. The father also put a family ring on his son's finger. The gift of the ring was an important sign of trust and of faith. The family ring bore an inset crest. The ring was dipped into hot wax and used to seal documents, but could also serve as a signature for monetary transactions. The father, in today's terms, would have given his son his credit card. The story is used to show the depth of God's love and forgiveness.

Each of these parables has something to do with the daily life of the people. The people could relate

Left: *The beauty of Galilee may have inspired many of Jesus' parables.*

many of the lessons to their own understanding of life.

Luke's Gospel reads, "Soon afterwards he went on through cities and villages, proclaiming and bringing the good news of the kingdom of God" (Luke 8:1). The Bible tells us that Jesus taught in towns, temple courtyards, on mountains, by the sea, and from boats on the lakes. Most of the parables told by Jesus reflect a location or a reality that was familiar to the people listening.

In New Testament biblical times, the difference between a town or city or village was established by its defenses, not by its size. If you lived in an unwalled settlement, you lived in a village. If you lived on a hill or a mount formed by the ruins of earlier

Below and opposite:
Gates were important in the defense of a city. These gates in Jerusalem, the Jaffa Gate (below) and the Zion Gate (right), fortified the city's entrances.

> *"Enter through the narrow gate; for the gate is wide and the road is easy that leads to destruction, and there are many who take it. For the gate is narrow and the road is hard that leads to life, and there are few who find it."*
> (Matthew 7:13-14)

settlements and the area had a surrounding wall, it was called a town. Frequently towns had a good water source nearby and their land was fertile. Often towns would be built at a crossroads or junction of main trading routes. In Jesus' day, the construction of towns reflected Greek and Roman influence. They had piped water, taller buildings, and public markets.

Moving in and out of towns and cities gave Jesus an opportunity to see how different towns or cities defended against possible attacks. Merchants carried their goods to market with human help or they had pack animals, such as donkeys or camels. To get into a town, you had to pass through a gate. Generally there would have been more than one gate or entryway into a town. A perfect gate would allow pack animals to fit through, but not be too much wider than that. If a gate were too wide and permitted simple entry and exit, invaders could easily disrupt the town life, steal the market goods, and be on their way. The most secure towns, the towns that offered a better life, were those with narrow gates.

This idyllic setting in Galilee was also the setting for many of Jesus' parables—it is easy to see the rocky soil and the fertile soil about which he preached.

In Matthew's Gospel we read about the two kinds of life within the community. One kind of person obeys the word of God and the other ignores it. Jesus used very concrete images to get his spiritual truth across to the people.

As with the parables, Jesus used examples from daily life to explain spiritual truths. Much of what Jesus talked about was hard to understand, and even his disciples, who were with him almost every day, did not understand every truth Jesus tried to explain.

Looking at the lush rolling green hills of Israel that are covered with plentiful orchards and vineyards, we see a beautiful image. However, the parables of Jesus frequently used the reality that much human toil and labor went into creating the beautiful farms, orchards, and vineyards, thus making the image even more poignant. In Matthew's Gospel, Jesus tells the parable of the Laborers in the Vineyard. Some of the laborers had worked hard all day and other laborers had worked only a few hours. Yet at the end of the day, the master paid every laborer the same full day's wage.

"Am I not allowed to do what I choose with what belongs to me? Or are you envious because I am generous? So the last will be first, and the first will be last."
(Matthew 20:15-16)

Both Matthew and Luke record the parable of the Lost Sheep. In this parable, Jesus asks his listeners for their opinion concerning the shepherd's choice to leave 99 sheep and go looking for one. Jesus concludes that if the shepherd found the lost sheep there would be greater rejoicing over this one than the 99 he had with him.

Jesus traveled much throughout the years he ministered and taught. But many of those towns and villages had little faith and so Jesus reproached them.

The scriptures note that Jesus was troubled because these towns that had heard his teachings did not show any change of heart or in their life. Even his hometown, Nazareth, and his adopted hometown, Capernaum, lacked faith in Jesus.

"Woe to you, Chorazin! Woe to you, Bethsaida! For if the deeds of power done in you had been done in Tyre and Sidon, they would have repented long ago in sackcloth and ashes."
(Matthew 11:21)

Though traveling in Jesus' time was difficult, Jesus continued to travel throughout Israel. Although there frequently were commercial travelers and religious pilgrims on the roads, journeys were rarely undertaken for pleasure, since most people traveled by foot. Provisions of food and water would not always be available and the danger of robbers was always present.

These dangers did not stop Jesus; he knew his fate and it was not to be killed by a robber on a road.

Jesus' stories and parables spread throughout the land. Even today, guides giving tours of Israel will often cite or read some of the parables that Jesus taught. And though some of the cultural facts have changed, Christians the world over still hold these stories in their hearts and try to live by their truths.

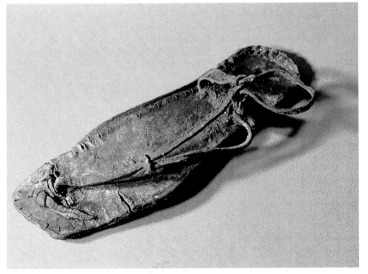

HIS DEATH AND RESURRECTION

❦

The crowds that went ahead of him and that followed him were shouting, "Hosanna to the Son of David! Blessed is the one who comes in the name of the Lord! Hosanna in the highest heaven!" When he entered Jerusalem, the whole city was in turmoil, asking, "Who is this?" The crowds were saying, "This is the prophet Jesus from Nazareth in Galilee." (Matthew: 21:9-11)

Left: *The Damascus Gate superimposed on the skyline of the city makes a beautiful picture.*
Right: *If you enter Jerusalem from this road on the Mount of Olives, it would lead you down to the Kidron Valley and then take you up to the Temple Mount.*

Jesus and his disciples traveled through Jericho on their journey to Jerusalem to celebrate Passover. The road from Jericho to Jerusalem climbs west into the mountains. The Jordan River is five to seven miles east of the town of Jericho. Jericho was an important city in Jesus' ministry and it is also where he taught one of the most important parables, the parable of the Good Samaritan.

The parable of the Good Samaritan is recorded in Luke. In the story, Jesus teaches about caring for everyone. The subjects of this parable are travelers on the road from Jerusalem to Jericho: a priest, a Levite, a Samaritan, and a wounded traveler. The priest and Levite see the beaten and wounded traveler on the road, but pass him by and offer no help. The Samaritan stops and cares for the victim, pouring oil and wine over the victim's wounds and bandaging them. He also pays for the victim's bill at a nearby inn.

Below and opposite: *The road from Jericho to Jerusalem is called Maale Adummim (in Hebrew it means the "red descent") because of the red stone throughout the hills. At the side of the main road stands the Inn of the Good Samaritan. These are not the remains of the original inn, nor is it sure that this is the exact location of the biblical inn. But people during Jesus' day would have traveled this way and there would have been an inn along this road.*

During Jesus' lifetime, the Samaritan people were the inhabitants of the central region of Palestine, between Judea and Galilee. They were a mixed race, who were descendants of the intermarriage of Israelites and Assyrian colonists. They were hated by the Jews. That Jesus would use a story of a compassionate Samaritan to illustrate his concept of being "neighborly" presented his listeners with a great challenge.

As Jesus and his disciples continued their journey to Jerusalem, a blind beggar shouted out repeatedly to him, "Jesus, Son of David, have mercy on me!" Jesus stopped, called the blind man forward, and asked what it was that he wanted of him. The man replied, "Lord, let me see again." Jesus responded, "Receive your sight; your faith has saved you." Luke records this in chapter 18, Mark in chapter 10, and Matthew in chapter 20 records that Jesus healed two blind men.

The interaction between Jesus and Zacchaeus, which took place in Jericho and is recorded in Luke 19, showed the people what Jesus believed was a proper attitude toward wealth. Zacchaeus was a chief tax collector, which was a despised profession. People bought from the Romans the right to collect taxes. Most Jewish

Opposite: Jericho is fed by a large spring, which makes it an oasis in the dry, hot desert. The spring is called the Spring of Elisha because Elisha purified the water by throwing salt into it.
Below: The agricultural aspects of the area were neglected after the ninth century. It has only been in the twentieth century that Jericho has again become a center of agriculture.

people bitterly resented this, because these tax collectors worked for the hated Romans, and the tax collectors were known to collect some of the money for themselves. Tax collectors were thought of as no better than robbers. The social position of tax collectors was low and they were ostracized. They were not eligible for public or religious office and they were not permitted to give evidence in Jewish courts. For Jesus to publicly express the salvation of Zacchaeus, by calling him forward and requesting to share a meal in his home, was another definite statement from Jesus that the "Son of Man came to seek out and to save the lost" (Luke 19:10).

Jericho has a very long history that reaches back thousands of years before Jesus to the lifetime of Abraham, Isaac, and Jacob. In Jericho, archaeologists have found numerous artifacts that they date as early as 6,000 B.C. The town of Jericho is located west of the Jordan River, approximately five miles from the north end of the Dead Sea. It has a freshwater spring that makes it an oasis in the surrounding desert.

Tourists in Jericho today travel about 900 feet below sea level and enjoy a vast array of palm trees as they pass through one of the oldest cities in the world. Jericho's winter climate is mild and this helps to make it a comfortable resort as well as making it a year-round source of fruits and vegetables.

Right: Jericho was the first city captured by the Israelites after they wandered in the desert for 40 years. Joshua led the victory with the sound of powerful trumpets and the walls of the city came tumbling down.

As Jesus and the disciples drew near to Jerusalem, the Bible notes that they came to the village of Bethphage on the Mount of Olives. Today, the village of Bethphage cannot be certainly identified. However, the hill east of Jerusalem known as the Mount of Olives remains. Tourists on the Mount of Olives are able to enjoy a magnificent view of the vast wilderness of Judea and the walled city of Jerusalem.

From Bethphage, Jesus sent two of his disciples to get him a donkey that had never been ridden before, on which he would ride into Jerusalem. They brought the donkey and laid their cloaks on it, and Jesus rode into the city. Others laid their cloaks on the ground in front of him, waving branches and singing his praises. He was greeted upon entering the city with singing and rejoicing. Even today, this event is celebrated by many Christians

as Palm Sunday. It would not be a full week before the same crowds would be demanding that Jesus be put to death on a cross.

In Matthew's Gospel, Jesus entered Jerusalem and went directly to the temple. There he saw people buying and selling sacrificial animals and changing money, and he became angry. He drove out all the merchants, and overturned the tables of the money changers.

Herod was building a great temple in Jerusalem. The walls were made out of limestone and the temple displayed the best architecture of the first century world. Jewish pilgrims traveled from all over to celebrate their great religious festivals in this temple.

Jewish records tell us that a major festival market operated in the Jerusalem temple and that those who sold goods paid heavy taxes. Jesus objected to the buying and selling of

Above: The view of Jerusalem from the far south hill of the Mount of Olives is breathtaking. The Dome of the Rock is a predominant sight.

sacrificial animals in the temple court, which was the only area available to non-Jews for worship.

But Jesus responded with compassion to the ill and the lame who had come to him in the temple, and he healed them. After performing his miracles of healing in the temple, Jesus "went out of the city to Bethany, and spent the night there" (Matthew 21:17). Bethany is a village about two miles from Jerusalem on the distant side of the Mount of Olives off the road to Jericho. It was in Bethany that Jesus stayed at the home of Mary and Martha and their brother Lazarus. In one of the most poignant stories in the Bible and one that seems to foreshadow Christ's own death and resurrection, Jesus raised Lazarus from the grave.

In Bethany, there were many date palm trees. Although the Bible does not mention the fruit of the palm tree, we do know that there were plenty of palm trees in Israel. The date palm is an elegant, graceful tree that can range from 80 to 100 feet tall. At this time, palm leaves were used as a national symbol of Israel's victories as well as to make baskets and to thatch roofs.

Throughout the Gospels, Jesus often went to Jerusalem for religious festivals. In fact, in John's Gospel many of Jesus' teachings are given in the courtyards of the Jerusalem temple. The main building of the temple was

Below: Bethany is a small village on the east slope of the Mount of Olives. This town has become well known because Jesus stayed with Simon the Leper before the Last Supper and Crucifixion. Opposite: Mary, Martha, and Lazarus lived in Bethany. This family, two sisters and a brother, were very dear friends of Jesus. The sisters called Jesus when their brother was ill, but Jesus did not arrive in time and Lazarus died. The tomb, from which Jesus raised him, is commemorated by this site.

Above: *The southwestern corner of the outer wall of Herod's Temple, or the Second Temple, as it appears today. The first temple was built by King Solomon on what is now known as the Temple Mount.*

Below: *A model of Herod's Temple at the Holy Land Hotel in west Jerusalem.*

constructed by King Herod the Great. However, for many years afterward, work on the temple continued. This temple was two times as large as the Temple of Solomon and it had so much gold that in the sunlight it was dazzling. Still in existence today is the great platform where the pilgrims gathered and sacrifices were offered. An area estimated to be 35 acres is enclosed by the walls of this platform. One of the southern ends of the platform, standing about 100 to 150 feet high, could be the pinnacle from which the devil tempted Jesus to throw himself down in Matthew 4:6.

In Jesus' day, there was a covered cloister around the outer courtyards of the temple. According to the Bible in the book of Acts, the two apostles Peter and John taught there after Jesus' death. The main entrance of the temple led to the Court of Gentiles and from there to the Court of Women. Women were not permitted to go into the inner sanctuaries of the temple itself. Men, however, could enter into the Court of Israel and for the Festival of Tabernacles they could enter into the Priests' Court for a procession around the altar. In Mark's Gospel, Jesus foretold the destruction of the temple.

Herod's Temple was destroyed at the time of the Jewish rebellion in A.D. 70 and its treasures were taken back to Rome.

Then Jesus asked him, "Do you see these great buildings? Not one stone will be left here upon another; all will be thrown down." (Mark 13:2)

———◇———

Over the centuries, Jerusalem has become a sacred symbol to many. Today, the wall that encircles the Old City is about two and a half miles long with seven open gates, and it offers tourists many breathtaking views from its ramparts. Each gate has a name and serves a specific purpose.

Above: An inscribed stone from Herod's Temple that forbade foreigners from entering the temple grounds. Below: These steps led to the Hulda Gate of Herod's Temple. Jesus may well have used these steps to enter the temple.

The Jaffa Gate is known in Arabic as *Bab el-Khalil*, or Gate of the Friend. It has an inscription over the entrance that reads, "There is no god but Allah and Abraham is his friend." In the late 1800s, Kaiser Wilhelm II visited Jerusalem. The Turks filled in the moat between the Jaffa Gate and the Citadel of David, trying to provide for the Kaiser's entry in a mounted procession. Today, this passage is used as a main thoroughfare for motor traffic going into the Old City.

Jerusalem's most ornate gate, and a fine example of Ottoman architecture, is the Damascus Gate, known in Arabic as *Bab el-Amud* (or Gate of the Column). According to the sixth century Madaba map of Jerusalem, there was a column inside the gate marking the northern gateway to the city.

Below: *The recently restored Damascus Gate is at the north entrance of Jerusalem. Recent excavations have revealed some remaining parts of the gate built during Roman times.*
Opposite: *The Jaffa Gate is the main entrance from the west. Pictured is the pedestrian entrance; the drive-through entrance is to the right.*

Nearest to Mount Moriah and to the Western Wall is the Dung Gate. This gate was named in the second century because the city's refuse was continually taken through the gate to be dumped outside the walls.

Herod's Gate faces the commercial center known as *Sheikh Jarrah*. The Gate was named Herod's Gate by medieval pilgrims who believed that just inside was the house of Herod Antipas.

The Lions Gate is called *Bab Sittna Miriam* by the Arabs. The road through this gate leads to Mary's Tomb. Christians since the Middle Ages have named this gate after Saint Stephen, who was martyred nearby.

Leading to Mount Zion is the Zion Gate. It is known to the Arabs as *Bab en Nabi Daoud*, or Gate of David the Prophet, because it allows access to the traditional tomb of King David.

To create an easier passageway between the Christian Quarter of the Old City and the developing Christian properties west of the gate, the New Gate was opened in 1887 by Sultan Abdul Hamid. People traveling in Jerusalem today are able to visit each of these gates.

Above: The Lions Gate faces the Mount of Olives. On each side of the entrance is a carved lion. It is believed that these lions represent the coat of arms of the Sultan Baybars.

Left: Herod's Gate is also called the Gate of Flowers. This gate leads into the Muslim Quarter.

The traditional site where Jesus and his disciples were thought to have stayed during their time in Jerusalem was in a building on Mount Zion, in a room above the ground floor. It is called the Cenacle, but is often called the Upper Room. It was while eating the Passover meal that Jesus announced that he would be betrayed by one of his own disciples. It was also at this meal that Jesus instituted the first Holy Communion, which is still celebrated by Christians to commemorate Christ's death and resurrection. Jesus also told Peter that he would deny Jesus three times before the cock next crowed.

After the Passover meal, Jesus and his disciples went to the Garden of

Above: *The Church of St. Peter in Gallicantu commemorates Peter's denial of Jesus three times before the cock crowed.*
Right: *The Cenacle, where the Last Supper was supposed to have taken place, is a twelfth century Crusader building on Mount Zion.*

Gethsemane. The name Gethsemane means oil press. This olive garden is located outside of Jerusalem and it is where Jesus spent some of his last hours. The garden is located on the western slope of the Mount of Olives. The olive tree is one of the most characteristic trees of Palestine. It thrives on dry limestone soil and has a gnarled trunk with silver-gray foliage. The olive tree requires a great deal of sunshine, but it does not require much

Below: Olives are still a plentiful fruit in Israel today. Opposite: The Garden of Gethsemane, with its ancient olive trees, is one of the most meaningful places for Christians. It was here that Christ agonized over his coming death.

"See, the hour is at hand, and the Son of Man is betrayed into the hands of sinners. Get up, let us be going. See, my betrayer is at hand."
(Matthew 26:45-46)

attention. It is a very strong tree. The olive is able to survive on hillsides where little else will grow and it lives a long time. Today, in the Garden of Gethsemane, there is a grove of ancient olive trees just like in Jesus' day.

The fruit of the olive tree had many uses in biblical times. The olives could be eaten in various ways; they provided oil for cooking and for lamps and the oil could be used to make ointments for wounds and for religious anointings. Olive oil was so plentiful that the surplus was exported. Olive branches remain a symbol of peace.

In Gethsemane, Jesus asked his disciples to wait for him. He took Peter, James, and John further into the garden and asked them to stay awake with him while he prayed. Three times he came back and found the three sleeping. The third time he found them sleeping, Judas approached him.

Judas gave the people following him a sign that told them which person to arrest. When Judas kissed Jesus, they knew whom to arrest. One of Jesus' disciples cut off a servant's ear, but Jesus told them to let the arrest happen. This event was a fulfillment of the Scriptures. Then all of Jesus' disciples ran off and deserted him.

It was probably here in the Garden of Gethsemane, on the eastern border of the Kidron Valley, that the disciples could not stay awake to wait for Jesus.

Above and right: The Basilica of the Agony, also known as the Church of All Nations, is in the Garden of Gethsemane. This church has an impressive mosaic on the front of the building, showing God looking down from heaven over Jesus and all the people of the world. Many nations contributed to the building of this church in 1924.

Right: On the Mount of Olives east of the Garden of Gethsemane is the Church of St. Mary Magdalene. It has decidedly Russian architecture, with its domes and crosses. It was built by Czar Alexander III in 1885, in memory of his mother, Maria Alexandrovna.

The remaining days of Jesus' life are commemorated weekly in Jerusalem. A continual flow of pilgrims and tourists travel the Via Dolorosa, which is the most sacred road of Christendom. There is no proof that this is the route Jesus took from the Antonia Fortress, where he was held prisoner, to Golgotha, where he was crucified. In fact, through the ages, there have been many different routes proclaimed as the "Way of the Cross," and even the number of stations of the cross has been changed many times. But the actual facts may not be as important as the truth that Jesus was in Jerusalem and that he did walk to his death there.

The Via Dolorosa starts where Jesus was condemned to die. It ends where he was buried in a nearby grave (or sepulchre). This current path is marked by 14 stations, the last 5 being within the Church of the Holy Sepulchre.

The Via Dolorosa begins in the ruins of the Antonia Fortress, where it is believed the Roman Procurator Pontius Pilate condemned Jesus. It was here that Pilate's legionaries mocked Jesus, crowned him with thorns, and gave him the purple robe to wear. Today this mocking and crowning with thorns are marked near the Monastery of the Flagellation, in the El-Omariye School courtyard. Every Friday, Christians reenact the "Way of the Cross" starting at this location.

Top left: *A model of the Antonia Fortress, where Christ was held prisoner.*
Bottom left: *The Chapel of the Flagellation was built over the traditional site where Christ was beaten by Roman soldiers. The church was built in 1839, and redesigned and rebuilt from 1927 to 1929.*

Above: The chapel of the Convent of the Sisters of Zion houses the right third of the Ecce Homo Arch. The arch was built under Hadrian's rule in A.D. 135.
Left: The third station marks Christ's first fall as he carried the cross to Golgotha. It is marked by a small chapel.

VITTORIA GISMONDI PELLEGRINA IN T.S. A RICORDO DEI SUOI GENITORI

Above: *Roman soldiers carved the dice games they played into the stones in front of the jail cells where prisoners were held. These stones may have been in front of the jail cell Jesus stayed in while in the Antonia Fortress.*

The present day Franciscan Compound holds three of the important stops of the "Way of the Cross." The compound is occupied by the El-Omariye School, the Franciscan Bible School with its beautiful Flagellation and Condemnation Chapels, and the Convent of the Sisters of Zion, which has valuable remains of the Antonia Fortress. The Chapel of the Flagellation, a medieval structure that was renovated in 1927 by Antonio Barlozzi, stands on the site of Jesus' scourging. The Chapel of Condemnation, a square structure of Byzantine form, marks the site where Pilate sentenced Jesus to death on a cross. The Convent of the Sisters of Zion houses an ancient arch that is believed to mark the site where Pilate said these words, "*Ecce homo*," to present Jesus to the crowd. The arch is appropriately named the Ecce Homo Arch.

Today, a Greek Orthodox monastery stands next to the Sisters of Zion Convent. In the basement of this monastery there remains part of the original Via Dolorosa as well as several caves probably used by the legionaries of Rome to stable their horses. One of the deepest caves in the monastery is marked as the "Prison of Barabbas." Barabbas was the prisoner released to the Jews during the feast of Passover when Jesus was apprehended.

Above: *The Ecce Homo Chapel dome is visible in this rooftop view of Jerusalem. At the right, in the far distance, you can see the golden dome of the Dome of the Rock.*
Opposite: *The middle third of the Ecce Homo Arch is visible in the street. Above, you can see the dome of the Ecce Homo Chapel.*

A nineteenth century Franciscan oratory stands on the spot where some think Simon of Cyrene was forced to carry the cross of Jesus. According to Mark's Gospel, Simon was the father of Alexander and Rufus, who were well known in the early Christian church. In Luke's Gospel, Jesus foretold the destruction of Jerusalem to the weeping women of Jerusalem who lined the road and watched Jesus' journey to Golgotha.

Golgotha, the "place of the skull" in Hebrew, is now covered by the Church of the Holy Sepulchre, possibly Christendom's most sacred shrine. Also in this church is the tomb where Jesus may have been laid, the stone where Jesus' body was anointed with oil after death, as well as an actual rock of Golgotha.

There is another possible site where Jesus was buried, and many Protestants believe this site is more accurate. The Garden Tomb, which is outside the north walls of the city, was found by the British general Charles Gordon in 1883. Today, Anglican Christians have turned it into a wonderful and inspiring devotional garden.

After Jesus was laid in the tomb provided by Joseph of Arimathea, and when the Sabbath was over, Mary and Mary Magdalene (Mark also adds Salome) went to Jesus' tomb to anoint him with spices, as was the Jewish custom. When they arrived, they did not find the body of Jesus. They were

Opposite: The Church of the Holy Sepulchre was, during the time of Christ, outside the walls of Jerusalem. The area was a quarry and the place for executions. This church has a long history, dating back to Constantine's basilica, which was consecrated in A.D. 335.

Above: Some people believe the Garden Tomb is the actual burial place of Jesus.
Below: This is the thirteenth station of the cross, the Stone of the Anointing, which is where Christ's body was anointed with spices and where his mother wept over his body.

instead greeted by angelic messengers who announced that Jesus had risen. In the Gospel of John, Jesus himself appears to Mary Magdalene.

Luke's Gospel records that a few of the apostles met Jesus on their way to the village of Emmaus. The apostles spoke and walked with Jesus for some time but did not know who he was. In fact, they did not know him until they stopped for the evening for supper. When Jesus blessed and broke the bread, the disciples recognized him. Emmaus was a village about eight miles west of Jerusalem. Today, the village of Emmaus may well be the Arab town Imwas, a village whose name still echoes Emmaus.

Jesus made many other appearances after the Resurrection. He appeared to Peter and the other apostles in Jerusalem in the Upper Room on Sunday evening, and he appeared to

Above and right: *The Church of the Holy Sepulchre was damaged by fire in 1808 and an earthquake in 1927. Beginning in 1959, restoration was done by many cooperating communities. Today, this church is shared by Roman Catholic, Greek Orthodox, Armenian, Coptic, Syrian, and Ethiopian churches.*

Top left: The Altar of the Stabat Mother at the Golgotha Chapel.

Top right: The last station of the cross is under the middle of the rotunda. The entrance to the tomb is through the Chapel of the Angel, which is where the angel was thought to have sat when he told the women Christ was no longer in the tomb.

Below: One of the many altars in the Church of the Holy Sepulchre. This one is at the last station of the cross.

Below: *The Mount of Olives is a holy place for Jews also, and is a favorite place to be buried. Jews believe that the Messiah will come to earth at the Mount of Olives and enter Jerusalem. Those buried on the mount will be the first to be raised to follow him.*

Right: *The Church of the Ascension is near the peak of the mountain. The church was built by Crusaders in the twelfth century, but has been a Muslim mosque since the thirteenth century.*

Opposite: *The Russian Church of the Ascension is at the summit of the Mount of Olives. Russian Christians believe the Ascension happened where the bell tower was placed.*

many others during the next 40 days. One week after Easter, Jesus came to talk to Thomas, who had missed his appearance the week before. Thomas had said he would not believe until he saw the marks of the nails in his hands. Jesus appeared and showed Thomas his marks and wounds.

Jesus made some other appearances after the Resurrection, including one to 500 people and one to 7 of the disciples fishing on the Sea of Galilee. But 40 days after the Resurrection, he ascended into heaven on the Mount of Olives. Luke is the only Gospel that tells us the story of the Ascension.

Today travelers and pilgrims may visit a small Crusader Chapel on the Mount of Olives that was built to commemorate the Ascension.

❧JERUSALEM TODAY❧

Jerusalem, Jerusalem, the city that kills the prophets and stones those who are sent to it! How often have I desired to gather your children together as a hen gathers her brood under her wings, and you were not willing! See, your house is left to you, desolate. For I tell you, you will not see me again until you say, 'Blessed is the one who comes in the name of the Lord.'" (Matthew 23:37-39)

Left: *The moonrise over the walls of Jerusalem creates a serene picture of a city that has seen much violence over hundreds of years.*
Above: *The Shrine of the Book houses the famous Dead Sea Scrolls.*

Below: *The Pool of Siloam is 1,600 feet long and the water is 10 to 16 inches deep. It is part of Hezekiah's Aqueduct.*

Opposite: *In about 700 B.C., King Hezekiah decided to insure a water supply inside the city walls of Siloam. The king engineered an S-shaped tunnel from Gihon to Siloam. Today tourists can follow this ancient tunnel approximately 600 yards from the Gihon Spring to the Pool of Siloam where it emerges.*

Following the Ascension, in the book of the Acts of the Apostles, Luke writes that the community of believers grew in their faith in Jesus as the Messiah, or Anointed One. Luke notes that the disciples of Jesus returned to Jerusalem to the Upper Room, also called the Cenacle, where they had been staying throughout Jesus' trial, crucifixion, burial, and resurrection. He writes about the disciple Peter organizing the followers of Jesus. One of Peter's first actions, according to Luke, was to tell the community about the fate of Judas, the betrayer.

Some believe that the Field of Blood, or "Potter's Field" as it is known, was purchased with the 30 pieces of silver that Judas earned for betraying Jesus. In Matthew's Gospel we read that Judas repented for his deed, and flung the 30 pieces of silver at the feet of the temple priests. The priests were unwilling to accept what they saw as "blood money" and so the money was used to purchase a burial place for strangers.

Today, Saint Onuphrius, a Greek convent, is built on the Field of Blood, a site that has many rock-hewn tombs, some from the first century. Also in this convent is a cave that has been named the "Cave of the Apostles." Some people think this cave is where the apostles of Jesus stayed during his trial.

Not far from Saint Onuphrius Convent is the Pool of Siloam. This pool is located at the end of Hezekiah's Tunnel off the Siloam Road. This pool marks the site of Jesus' miraculous curing of the man born blind that is recorded in John's Gospel. Today, this site is marked by a small modern mosque.

Hezekiah's Tunnel dates back to the rule of King Hezekiah, about 700 B.C. Archaeological evidence indicates that the tunnel was dug by people working on opposite ends who met in the middle. Its purpose was to allow the water of Gihon Spring, which was outside the city walls, to channel to Siloam inside the city walls.

Jerusalem, the capital city of Israel, has a history of approximately four

thousand years. While it is sometimes called the City of Peace, there is no city that has been fought over as often as Jerusalem. Arabs, Jews, Babylonians, British, Byzantines, Crusaders, Jordanians, Mamelukes, Macedonians, Seleucids, Seljuks, and Turks are only some of the conquerors whose names are listed in Jerusalem's anguished past.

Jerusalem has a role in world history of greater proportion than its geographic size and economic importance would dictate. Today, Jerusalem is recognized as a sacred city by the world's Christians, Jews, and Muslims. For Christians, Jerusalem is where Jesus was crucified. For Jews, Jerusalem is where King David built his capital and Solomon constructed God's Temple. To Muslims, it is where Muhammad made his leap to heaven.

Over the centuries, more than a billion people have come to recognize Jerusalem as a sacred symbol. The ground of Jerusalem is the foundation for many shrines venerated by the three great monotheistic religions. While Jerusalem has known much struggle and change, the city has maintained its strength and spirit.

The Dome of the Rock is at Mount Moriah, a rocky Judean knoll. Many believe that it was here that Abraham presented his only son Isaac for sacrifice. The rock crowning the summit of Mount Moriah was Abraham's altar to God, and David later may have placed the Ark of the Law there. Solomon, David's son, built a beautiful temple on Moriah, which was destroyed by Nebuchadnezzar in 587 B.C.

Above: *The tile work on the outside of the Dome of the Rock is a floral mosaic pattern.*

In the early years of Christianity, Moriah was looked at as a place cursed by God. With the growth of Christianity, the Mount gradually deteriorated until it became a heap of desolate rubble. In A.D. 639, the forces of Islam overpowered Jerusalem and Moriah became a Muslim shrine. It is said that Muhammad made his leap to heaven from this rock, which is now enshrined in one of the most important and beautiful mosques in the world. In 1099, the mosque was overtaken by Crusaders and the Dome of the Rock became Christianity's Temple of the Lord. One century later, the golden cross that adorned the temple was thrown to the earth and the star and crescent replaced it. Ever since, Mount Moriah has been a Muslim shrine.

Opposite top: The Dome of the Rock is covered in tiles from Persia and marble. Arabic script runs along the upper edge of the octagon.
Opposite bottom left: The golden dome is made of an aluminum bronze alloy from Italy.
Opposite bottom right: The inside of the Dome is beautiful red, black, and gold stucco. The base is golden and inscribed with verses from the Koran. There are also glorious stained-glass windows surrounding the interior dome with intricate mosaic abstractions of corn, grapes, date palms, and fruit.

Above: *The Citadel Museum is marked by this arch. The museum is near the Jaffa Gate.*
Right: *The Sound and Light Show at the Jerusalem City Museum by the Citadel of David is beautiful.*
Opposite: *The Western Wall is the only remaining part of the Second Temple, which was destroyed by the Romans in* A.D. *70. It is also called the Wailing Wall, because Jews have gone there to pray and grieve the destruction of Herod's Temple.*

One of Jerusalem's most prominent landmarks is the Citadel, at the west entrance to the Old City. It marks the fortified gateway built by Herod the Great next to his personal palace. Today, this area is used for cultural and educational exhibitions. Some of the excavations within the Citadel have been marked by the Department of Antiquities, and from the top of David's Tower you can see the extent of Herod's Palace, which covered the area presently used by Christ Church, the police barracks, and the northern half of the Armenian Quarter. Christ Church draws many tourists. It has two granite columns that are thought to have come from Egypt to decorate Herod's Palace.

The police barracks south of the Citadel, on the site of Herod's Palace, is where the three Magi would have presented themselves to inquire about the newborn king of the Jews.

The Armenian Compound is located on Mount Zion. The Armenian people were the first nation in the world to embrace Christianity. Their compound is almost a city; it contains schools; quarters for teachers, pupils, pilgrims, and the patriarch; a seminary; museum; library; printing press; and a monastery. Within the compound is the Mardigian Museum that contains a collection of the patriarchate's treasures. However, the Compound is best known for its ancient Saint James Cathedral.

The Cathedral is associated with two saints, both called James. James the Fisherman, or Saint James "the Greater," was one of Jesus' 12 apostles. He was beheaded by the grandson of Herod the Great, Herod Agrippa. The other James was known·as Saint James "the Less." He became the first bishop of Jerusalem. In A.D. 60, he was thrown from the temple pinnacle into the Kidron Valley where he was stoned and was buried. The main altar in the Cathedral is dedicated to James the Less, who is buried beneath it. The base of the walls and the pillars in the Cathedral are covered with ceramic glazed antique tiles, which are painted in the Armenian style.

Opposite: St. James Cathedral is located in the Armenian Convent of the Armenian Quarter. It is the largest and most revered Armenian church.
Below: The Armenian Quarter offers visitors many things beside rich history and St. James Cathedral. The richest resource most visitors find is the people.

Above: *The Old City of Jerusalem is defined by the walls and streets laid out in the sixteenth century by Suliman the Magnificent. Its markets give us a glimpse of what medieval life was like.*

Another interesting site in the Armenian Compound is the traditional site of the House of Annas. According to John's Gospel, Jesus was taken to Annas, the father-in-law of the high priest, before being led to the Sanhedrin for judgment. There is an olive tree in the northeastern corner of the chapel that is said to be the tree to which Jesus was tied while waiting for Annas. Today, travelers enter this chapel by passing through a beautiful portico.

One of the finest examples of Crusader construction in the Holy Land is the old and beautiful Church of Saint Anne in Jerusalem. It is believed that in a small cave in the northeast of the temple compound was the home of Joachim and Anna, the parents of Mary, the grandparents of Jesus. Excavators have found the remains of an extremely ancient pool west of the church. The pool is identified as the Pool of Bethesda. In John's Gospel, this pool is the place where Jesus healed a man who had been crippled for 38 years. The Bethesda Pool was rectangular and surrounded on all four sides by porches, and divided laterally by a fifth porch. The historian Eusebius wrote that one of the pools was used to wash the sheep before sacrificing them in the temple. Today, visitors can enjoy a biblical museum established by the White Fathers near Saint Anne's Church. This museum exhibits many interesting archaeological items found in the area.

In the Christian Quarter, tourists will discover monasteries, schools, missions, hospices, churches, souvenir shops, and historic and holy places. Although there are many domes and spires, the spire of the Lutheran Redeemer Church is the most dominant. Also located in this quarter is the Greek Orthodox Church of John the Baptist. Associated with the Greek Orthodox Church is a convent library that has a valuable collection of ancient and historic manuscripts.

Left: *West of St. Anne's Church is the excavated area of the Bethesda Pool.*
Below: *The New Gate leads to the entrance of the Christian Quarter in the Old City of Jerusalem.*

The modern city of Jerusalem offers tourists a number of museums, large and small. The Israel Museum, constructed in 1965, is a modern structure. Today, there are four separate museums. The Bezalel Museum of Art and Folklore has many objects of Jewish folk art, including Hanukkah lamps, Torah scroll sheaths, and a colorful collection of costumes and jewelry. There is also a *mih rab*, a Muslim prayer niche that faces Mecca. The second museum is the Bronfman Archaeological and Antiquities Museum. The exhibits here cover hundreds of years, from the Stone Age to the Ottoman period. A very popular exhibit is the Bar Kochba revolt. This exhibit contains objects from caves in the Judean desert near the Dead Sea where a small group of Jewish warriors and their families defied the power of Rome in A.D. 132.

In the Billy Rose Art Garden, the third museum, there are many statues and sculptures placed throughout the artificial semicircular rock terraces designed by Isamu Naguchi, a Japanese landscape artist. The fourth museum in this complex is the Shrine of the Book. Here the famous Dead Sea Scrolls are kept as well as the Bar Kochba letters and some scroll fragments from Masada.

The Rockefeller Museum, also known as the Palestine Archaeological Museum, stands on the grounds where Godfrey de Bouillon's Crusaders advanced against Jerusalem in 1099. This museum includes items dating from prehistoric through medieval times. One of its remarkable features is its reading room. The room contains over 100 periodicals and more than 35,000 volumes dealing with the archaeology, geography, and the history of the Holy Land.

Near the entrance to Mount Herzl stands the Herzl Museum, which contains photographs, letters, books, and various items associated with Theodor Herzl's life. Herzl, a journalist,

Right: *The Monastery of the Holy Cross, built in the fifth century, once stood outside Jerusalem, but is now surrounded by the expanded city. Because of its isolated location, it fell victim to many of the groups that invaded the city and has needed many repairs. The Israel Museum is in the background.*
Opposite: *The Rockefeller Museum contains many examples of Omayad art, architecture, and sculpture.*

Right: *The Yad Vashem monument was completed in 1957 and this sculpture stands outside it. The floor of the monument has randomly placed name plaques identifying different death camps.*

developed an interest in the plight of the Jews after attending the Dreyfus trial in Paris that exposed French anti-Semitism. In 1847, Herzl organized the First Zionist Congress in Basle. This proved to be a major step toward reconstructing the spirit of Jewish nationhood. North of the museum are the tombs of Herzl's family and a military cemetery. Northwest of the museum is a Holocaust Memorial and the Yad Vashem, a monument erected in memory of European Jews who were murdered in World War II. Leading to this memorial is a tree-lined path titled Avenue of the Righteous. All the trees here were planted by non-Jews who had risked their lives to help Jews escape from the Nazis.

The Taxation Museum is one of two such existing museums in the world. It deals entirely with taxation. It has exhibits illustrating methods of taxation and collection in ancient Israel, the Diaspora, and in Israel City.

No one knows exactly how Israel looked some 2,000 years ago. However, archaeologists and researchers continue to provide us with information that allows us to walk where those before us walked and to see what they saw. Israel, and especially Jerusalem, continue to fascinate both believers and nonbelievers. Whether you go as a pilgrim or just as a tourist, but probably as a little of both, you will be impressed with the history and beauty of the Holy Land.

Right: A view of Jerusalem on the road from Bethlehem.

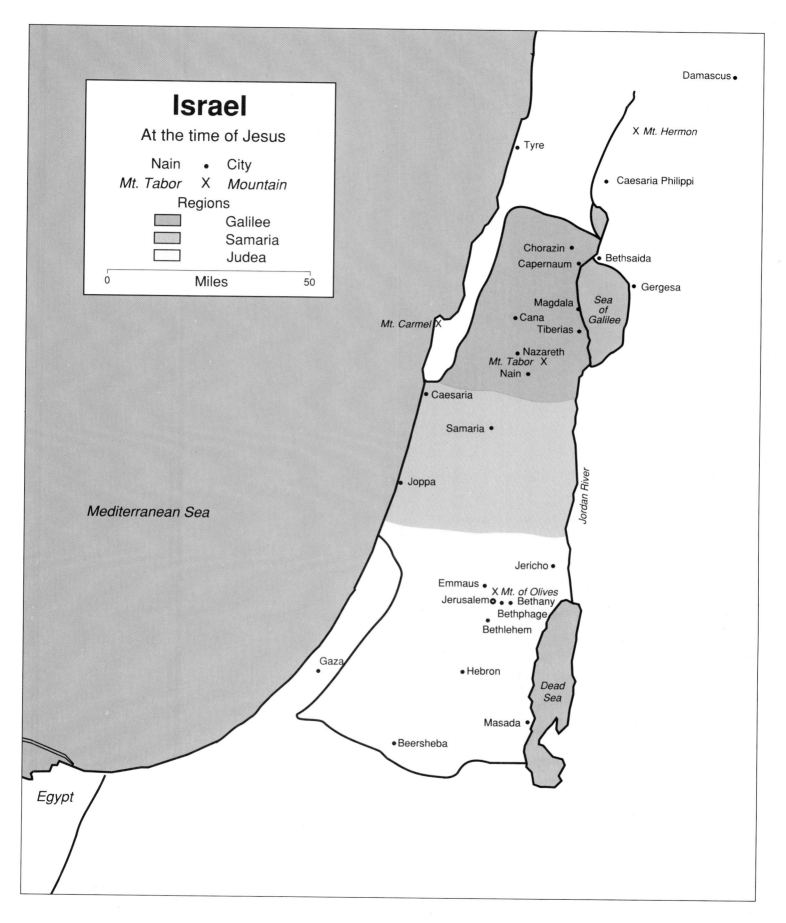

Israel

At the time of Jesus

Nain   •   City
Mt. Tabor   X   *Mountain*

Regions

Galilee
Samaria
Judea

0   Miles   50

Damascus •

X *Mt. Hermon*

• Tyre

• Caesaria Philippi

Chorazin •
Capernaum •   • Bethsaida

Sea of Galilee

• Gergesa

Magdala
• Cana
Tiberias

Mt. Carmel X

• Nazareth
Mt. Tabor   X
Nain   •

• Caesaria

Samaria •

Mediterranean Sea

• Joppa

Jordan River

Jericho •

Emmaus •
    X *Mt. of Olives*
Jerusalem ○ •   • Bethany
Bethphage

• Bethlehem

Gaza •

• Hebron

Dead Sea

Masada •

• Beersheba

Egypt

127

☙ INDEX ☙